Nettles

Luisa Futoransky

Nettles

translated from Spanish
by
Philippa Page

Shearsman Books

First published in the United Kingdom in 2016 by
Shearsman Books
50 Westons Hill Drive
Emersons Green
BRISTOL
BS16 7DF

Shearsman Books Ltd Registered Office
30–31 St. James Place, Mangotsfield, Bristol BS16 9JB
(this address not for correspondence)

www.shearsman.com

ISBN 978-1-84861-464-2

Copyright © Lisa Futoransky, 2010
Translations copyright © Philippa Page, 2016
Introduction copyright © Jason Weiss, 2016

The right of Lisa Futoransky to be identified as the author of this work,
and of Philippa Page to be identified as the translator thereof
has been asserted by them in accordance with the
Copyrights, Designs and Patents Act of 1988.
All rights reserved.

Ortigas was first published in Argentina in 2010
by Editorial Leviatán, Buenos Aires.

Contents

Introduction	6
Jubileo romano	10
Roman Jubilee	11
Con los dedos	16
With the Fingers	17
Puchero	22
Pauper's Stew	23
Dolesme	24
Hurt(s) Me	25
Rueca con violácea	26
Spinning Wheel with Violet	27
Sistema de sistemas	28
System of Systems	29
Cotillón	30
Cotillion	31
Excarificaciones	34
Scarifications	35
Hora del lobo: reliquia andina	36
Hour of the Wolf: Andean Relic	37
Amanece tormenta de julio en el balcón	38
July Storm As Dawn Breaks on the Balcony	39
Ios, la chiquita	40
Ios, the Little One	41
Érase, Belle Isle	42
Once upon Belle Isle	43
Cielito lindo	50
Cielito lindo	51

Crónicas / Chronicles

Cuarteto de Praga	66
Prague Quartet	67
Ortigas de Saorge	82
Nettles from Saorge	83
Gambier, Ohio	96
Gambier, Ohio	97

Introduction

Inveterate traveller since her earliest wanderings, Luisa Futoransky draws from a deep well. A long-distance poet, she listens to the world with the instincts of a diviner, ready to cull its ineffable moments and render them in a few lines where they will bloom again. Like a Chinese ink painter, with the merest of means and a free hand she sketches ancient histories, migrations, tales of hope and heartbreak, and word by word—exact, deliberate, chosen words—brings us to the point of insight. Her poems stand us upright somehow amid the dizzying swirl of existence, even as they reflect the many places she has known.

I first met Luisa soon after she landed in Paris some 35 years ago, where she still lives. Often I marvelled at how she got along: not that poetry meant a vow of poverty, not quite, but from her modest employments, the occasional grants and invitations, the humble abode that was her home, she learned to spin a kind of gold; richer than gold, more enduring, made with just what was at hand, small nothings, words. It took me a long time to appreciate the distillation that was going on. Her erudition, then as now, she wore lightly and the humour with which she faced every reversal and revelation had a seasoned quality that seemed well earned.

But where did she come from, and how did she gain such fluency with the ways of the world? Born and raised in Buenos Aires, from an Eastern European Jewish immigrant family, she studied music and literature and received her law degree from the university there. During the 1960s, after working under Borges at the national library, she travelled extensively throughout Latin America and left Argentina permanently in 1971, when she was a guest at the Iowa Writers Workshop. Following that, she lived in Spain and Rome, with several visits to Israel, and for four years taught opera in Japan. In the late 1970s, she moved to Beijing, working in the Spanish language bureau of the Chinese state radio. From there, in 1981, she moved to Paris.

For most of her first dozen years in Paris, she worked as an art museum guard at the Centre Pompidou. Eventually she found a position at the Agence France Presse, part of a venerable tradition among Latin American writers in Paris. Another decade and a half, she reached mandatory retirement age, though she continues to write, edit, and translate for UNESCO's magazine. And all the while, of course, every couple of years, she published another book. Next year, her publisher in Buenos Aires, Leviatán, will bring out her collected poems, fifty-plus years after her first book.

Luisa established herself initially as a poet with several books in the '60s and '70s. After settling in Paris she took up prose as well. Since then, five novels and two non-fiction books (on hair and honeymoons) have appeared, along with at least fifteen books of poetry. She is a poet of lived experience above all, though not hers alone; other voices inhabit the work, whether of friends, lovers, fellow travellers (people she met or figures from history and literature). Like the poetry, her fiction employs a direct language rooted in anecdote and reflection, while sometimes delighting in playful experimentalism. Hers are mosaic narratives, made of pieces, fragments.

Something else to notice in *Nettles* is her flair for the theatrical, especially acute when she writes in shorter forms. Surely her studies of opera helped to hone her instinct for the dramatic gesture. But to think that we start in Rome with this book only to end up in Ohio. That is some sense of humour.

JASON WEISS
translator of Luisa Futoransky's
The Duration of the Voyage: selected poems
(Junction Press, New York, 1997)

ORTIGAS

NETTLES

Jubileo romano

Ocre, rosa, naranja enigmas,
sabores romanos
que el cuerpo revisita
deleitándose en jirones de antiguos sobresaltos
y repentinas languideces

sin violencia el sol te acompaña la jornada
y por la noche discutimos la transparencia
en la poesía de Mario Luzi
o la intensidad minuciosa del dolor en Umberto Saba

los voluntarios del jubileo suben y jadean escalinatas
con chalecos de fuerza azul índigo
y ribetes amarillos de justa deportiva
de espaldas a cuanto corre
o se estanca en el légamo del Tíber

gladiadores de cartón piedra
nuevos restoranes
de incierta sonrisa y calidad
y tanto *buona sera*
Roma, la sardónica
tan fiel en amistad

Roman Jubilee

Ochre, rose, orange
riddles, Roman flavours
that the body rediscovers
taking delight in the remnants of ancient upheavals
and sudden languor

without violence the sun accompanies your day
and in the evening we discuss transparency
in the poetry of Mario Luzi
or the meticulous intensity of pain in Umberto Saba

volunteers of the jubilee puff and pant their way up staircases
in indigo straightjackets
trimmed like sportswear with yellow ribbon
their backs turned to where life flows
or stagnates in the Tiber's silt

papier-mâché gladiators
new restaurants
of an uncertain smile and quality
and so much *buona sera*
sardonic Rome
so loyal in friendship

2

A las butacas semi vacías
de un cine al aire libre llegan
los lamentos de los tarantulados del Cilento
las canciones en guikro
un cantautor mañoso y ronco
trashumantes, los saltimbanquis recorren la península
las mesas, los vinos, los adioses
los hoteles y sudores de una noche
¿para ya no más volver?

montaña con montaña no podrán acercarse
pero la gente que es tan pero tan pequeña
quién sabe sí

2

Into the half-empty seats
of an open-air cinema
enter the convulsions of tarantula-like dancers from Cilento
songs in *guikro*
a hoarse and wily singer
roving jugglers make their way along the peninsula
tables, wines, goodbyes
hotels and the fever of a one night stand
to never again return?

one mountain can never get any closer to another
but people, who are so very small
perhaps might, who knows

3

mariposas amarillo acidulado
diminutas
otras más negro que siena
tiesas, grandes, muy recamadas
pero que siempre cabrán en la palma
que jamás osará cazarlas
que no es tarea de buena gente
andar cortando alas

van y vienen entre campanillas azul intenso
con grutas al fondo
por donde nace infancia
con gotas nuevas de rocío
todavía

irse de aquí con el *corpo feixado*
en un buen trabajo de hechicero pernambucano
que me haga impune a los dolores
pero no invisible
ni tampoco piedra

alma la mi alma
dame la mano
que más allá del Tíber
no respondo
dame tregua
de una vez

3

tiny
acidic yellow butterflies
others blacker than Siena
stiff, large, very embroidered
but that always fit inside the palm
that will never dare hunt them
it's not the task of good people
to go around clipping wings

they come and go between the bluebells
caves in the background
where childhood is reborn
still covered
with drops of fresh morning dew

to leave here with *corpo feixado* [1]
from a good spell cast by a Pernambucan shaman
may it render me immune against the pains
although not invisible
or made of stone

soul of my soul
lend me your hand
for beyond the Tiber
I do not respond
grant me a truce
once and for all

---

[1] *corpo feixado* literally means 'closed body', used in a supernatural sense as a means of making the body impervious to evil or harm.

Con los dedos

qué se espera de un viejo? que pida turno con especialistas
que le confirmarán por si falta le hacía
el deterioro irremediable

que mate el tiempo
que sus deseos como él se jubilen sin júbilo de la vida del paso y el respiro
sus allegados, la ciudad, se vengan de sus antiguas perrerías y petulancia
le multiplican escaleras
veredas jabonosas
apenas con un alfiler
un martillito de viento le quiebran la dentadura postiza
en el lavabo del hotel
y para rematarla los duendes de la noche la tiran por la ventana
y el vecindario se queja por ruidos molestos
intempestivos
joder con los viejos
hay quien dice que huelen tan mal como los linyeras
o los muros de las prisiones
porque el olor de una clase de adolescentes en verano
voltea marea

distinto

With the Fingers

what can be expected of an old boy? That he books an appointment with
    specialists
merely for them to confirm his irredeemable deterioration
as if he really needed to be told

that he's killing time
that his desires like him are retiring without rapture from a life of stepping
    forth and drawing breath
his kin, the city, take revenge for his dirty old tricks and petulance

stairs multiply in front of him
soapy pavements
barely a pin
a little hammering of the wind break his dentures
in the hotel sink
and just to finish them off the night elves hurl them out of the window
and the neighbours complain about the unearthly racket
damn these old codgers
some say they smell as foul as tramps
or prison walls
because the stench of a class of adolescents in summertime
turns one's stomach

but in a different way

el viejo vive en un inmenso país de gente resfriada
por el arrepentimiento y los tiempos condicionales
un país de peter pan
de principitos destronados y cochambrosos
que la parsimonia con que abren sus chequeras no ventila

país de excrecencias, temblores, toses
alfombrado de pesadillas
yo lázaro transmito
al volver de la academia
tradición obliga
preciosos mendrugos, edictos de cariño

el arcoiris se come con los dedos
el rocío aminora el mal aliento
las piedras preciosas en los bolsillos dificultan el vuelo
soltarlas en el firmamento lo aligeran

the old man lives in a vast country of people congested
with repentance and conditional times
a country of Peter Pan
of filthy, dethroned little princes
the stinginess with which they open their chequebooks won't redeem them

country of excrescences, tremors, coughs
carpeted with nightmares
upon my return from the academy
I, Lazarus, impart
as tradition obliges
precious crusts, edicts of affection

the rainbow is to be eaten with the fingers
dew abates bad breath
carrying precious stones in pockets hinders flight
letting go of them in the sky alleviates

descifrar alfabetos en la forma de las nubes desempolva la penuria
tirar del cántaro
hasta que por fin se rompa
en una luminosa astilladura de partículas
para qué otra cosa están hechos acaso los cántaros
la gente
las medias las casas
los elefantes
sino para romperse
así
de repente
y a sabiendas

deciphering alphabets in the shapes made by the clouds dusts off the penury
skating on thin ice
until it finally shatters
into a bright explosion of particles
for what other reason are things
people
socks
houses
elephants
made
but to be broken
just like that
all of a sudden
and knowingly

Puchero

los del trópico de capricornio
que me tendieron de espaldas entre las sábanas
más o menos ásperas, grises a fuerza de nubes
que amenazan falsa lluvia
y plegadas a la que me importa
se hicieron con la mejor parte de esperanza
pájaro que denigró
voló

el resto, zarpa desprolija de carroñeros
y monederos falsos
tuvo que contentarse con despojos de sangre, lava
y escupir, para no atorarse
los huesos de por aquí

sin embargo amanezco sin mayor nostalgia
con el rabo del ojo miro las lápidas
y estragos con que el tiempo me vengó

sabrosos, chicos
me quedan para el puchero
ramito de hierbas, bien fragantes
hueso de chiquizuela
y delicado
el añejo caracú

Barrio XIII, París, 9.3.09

Pauper's Stew

those from the Tropic of Capricorn
who reached out to me whilst my back was pressed against the rather
        coarse
bed sheets, turned grey by the clouds
that threaten false rain
and tousled any old how
they made away with the best part of hope
cupboard love

the rest, a dishevelled pack of scavengers
and false wallets
had to be content with the residue of blood, lava
and to spit out, so as not to choke
on the bones from around here

I arouse, however, without great nostalgia
take a wry glance out of the corner of my eye at the headstones
and the ravages with which time took its revenge upon me

juicy fellows
you're all left over for my stew
sprig of herbs, nice and fragrant
a bone for stock
and delicate
mature bone marrow

13th Arrondissement, Paris, 9.03.09

Dolesme

una corneja atrapa
en el piso de lajas
una viborita
la revolea
la deja caer asestándole un golpe
repite el gesto hasta que la mata
y se la come

algo deja
y lo sube a la hembra que atenta
espera en el alero

hembra digo
porque no sé distinguir
el sexo de las cornejas
tampoco
el de la gente

finalmente
todo es pérdida

olvídame
que yo no puedo

Hurt(s) Me

a crow catches
a small viper
on the sandstone ground
spins it around
lets it fall dealing it a blow
repeats the gesture until it has been killed
and eats it

he leaves some
and takes it up to the female who awaits
patiently in the eaves

I say female
because I know not how to tell
the sex of a crow
neither
that of people

finally
everything is loss

forget me
as I cannot

Rueca con violácea

Helena tenía una droga contra el llanto y la cólera
que hacía olvidar todos los males.

Una larga temporada yo iba –haciendo de hazmerreír a no sé cuantos–, a la terminal de autobuses que venían de San Pablo y Curitiba: vos te habías ido porque estabas enamorado –proclamabas–, de una jovencita llamada Yara Amerildo Pimentel y cuando ni recibirte quiso, volviste. Pero esa noche no había ido a esperarte.

No rueca con violácea lana.
No árbol de mil escudos, no raíces para revigorizar el olvido
Hojarasca de urbe, puro amianto el viento nos dejó.

Spinning Wheel with Violet

Helen possessed a drug against sobbing and fury
which made her forget all evils

For a long time, I would go down to the terminus where buses would arrive from São Paulo and Curitiba—making a laughing stock out of myself in front of I don't know how many: you'd left—you would proclaim—because you were in love with a young girl called Yara Amerildo Pimentel and when she didn't even want to open up her door to you, you came back. But that night, I had not been to wait for you.

No spinning wheel with violet wool.
No tree of a thousand shields, no roots to reinvigorate the oblivion
Fallen urban leaves, sheer asbestos left to us by the wind.

Sistema de sistemas

Dolor rodilla dolor tobillo
dolor encía
Columnas que se doblan
quiebran
tristes juncos
Dolor mapa de reconocimiento
palanca
Mi dolor mueve los gusanos de este mundo
¿Soy, estoy o parezco
enferma?

System of Systems

Knee pain ankle pain
gum pain
Spines that twist
sad reeds
break
Pain a map of reconnaissance
crowbar
My pain stirs the worms of this world
Am I, am I just for now or do I merely appear
ill?

Cotillón

como todo muerto de a poco o de golpe
me voy de tu memoria
primero mi cara de antes
después la de ahora
por andrajos, rastros de mi voz
ni con clavel recién cortado en la solapa
me reconocerías

de las nubes volverán algunas lágrimas
necesarias para forjar una estatuilla de Bajo Congo
con espejo de azogue cuarteado,
pelos de pubis, clavos herrumbrados, dientes
que no asusta siquiera al dueño de la tienda

en estos lugares raros a mediodía
hace más frío que al amanecer
y nunca sale el sol

Cotillion

like any person who has died, little by little or suddenly
I leave your memory
first the face I used to have
then the one I wear now
not by the rags, traces of my voice
or freshly-picked carnation in my lapel
would you recognize me

some tears will return from the clouds
those necessary to forge
with a cracked mercury mirror
pubic hairs, rusty nails, teeth
a statuette from the Lower Congo
that doesn't even frighten the shopkeeper

in these strange places at midday
it is colder than at dawn
and the sun never shines

ahora
nos damos besos de viento como saludo
para decir nada.
¿Amor, acaso este viaje desorbitado?
En el mejor de los casos un juego de autitos que se chocan
en el parque de diversiones, ¿quién pasa la corriente,
quién la corta? ¿Quién cobra entrada? ¿Y cuando no hay más
dinero para comprar vueltas?
Se cambia de juego.
Se vuelve a casa.
¿Qué, pero qué casa?

La del desierto
de luz excesiva, de verdad, puro duna
sin matorrales ni bichitos.
Eternidad de pacotilla
la playa está
redentora
húmeda de grisáceos, pegajosos

improperios

now
we greet each other with kisses in the air
so as to say nothing
Is love by any chance this exorbitant journey?
Or in the best case scenario a game of bumper cars
at the fairground, who's controlling the electric current?
Who's cutting it off? Who's charging admission? And once there's no more
    money to have another go, what then?
Change game.
Go home.
But to *what* home?

The one in the desert,
of excessive light, of truth, pure sand dune
no scrub or bugs whatsoever
Second-rate eternity
the beach is
conciliatory
festering with clammy, greyish

insults

Escarificaciones

una fecha en tiza
agua de borrajas
un pulóver verde
una pollera cortona de gros ajustada negra
qué zapatos
qué pisadas
un registro civil
hace más de medio siglo

y vos guitarreando
hasta que las derrotas se hicieron nudos de olivo viejo

así de simple
se nos anegaron los sueños
y astillaron las utopías

¿de esos barros
estos lotos?

un negocio sin pérdida
a tiempo completo
es la tienda de borrar tatuajes
descontando que las escarificaciones
con tinta invisible
y pura savia
siempre quedan

Scarifications

a date in chalk
dead in the water
a green jumper
a tight black grosgrain skirt
which shoes
which footprints
a registry office
more than half a century ago

and you strumming on your guitar
until the defeats became knots on an old olive tree

it's that simple
our dreams were swamped
and our utopias splintered

do these lotuses really bloom
from those quagmires?

a shop that could erase tattoos
would be a sure-fire
full time business
except that scarifications
from invisible ink
and pure sap
always remain

Hora del lobo: reliquia andina

con esfuerzo, al amanecer, algunas veces las nubes
me dejan ver entre dos torres
un rectángulo donde emerge, soberano, el *sumaq urcu*
del huayna potosí
en pleno modesto barrio trece de parís estoy –quiera o no
aunque la borre con el codo, veinteañera, en bolivia
y cuando llega aurora solloce quedo, desafinada

qué hago con las vetas, qué hago con las venas y las velas
que dejé en la casa de moneda
mi bastón de mando en el cristo de la caña
mis pies, la sonrisa entregada en el portal de san francisco
polvo y chicha me fermentan la palabra
fijate que arde el predio, estaqueada
de memoria
qué hago
sin mí

Hour of the Wolf: Andean Relic

with a little effort, at dawn, the clouds sometimes
let me catch sight of
a rectangle in which the *sumaq urcu*, sovereign
of the Huayna Potosí, emerges
in between two towers
in the middle of the modest 13th arrondissement in Paris I am—like it
    or not
even if I erase it with my elbow—a twenty-something once again in Bolivia
and when dawn breaks I let out a muffled sob, out of tune

what should I do with the veins of silver, what should I do with my own
    veins and the candles
that I left at the mint
my sceptre in the Christ of the Sugar Cane
my feet, the smile turned in at the gateway to San Francisco
dust and *chicha*[1] fermented my words
take note that the land is burning, my memory
stretched out between the stakes
what to do
without me

---

[1] *Chicha* is the name given to a variety of fermented and non-fermented drinks in South and Central America. Whilst it is most commonly derived from maize, it can also be made from a range of other fruit, root vegetables or grains.

Amanece tormenta de julio en el balcón

huele a tormenta de verano
a rayos y centellas
a eclipse

quien dice rosal
dice bichos
y de vos
ni un fósil me quedó

¿los pañuelitos con los que pavarotti
cantaba que me amabas
quién los heredó?

lo verdadero es el sabor a trueno
a lágrima enterrada
a gusano

y el aroma del café

July Storm As Dawn Breaks on the Balcony

it smells of summer storm
of sheets and forks of lightning
of an eclipse

she who utters rose bush
also evokes greenfly
and of you
not even a fossil remains

the handkerchiefs with which Pavarotti
would sing that you loved me
who inherited those?

what's real is the taste of thunder
of buried tears
of maggot

and the scent of coffee

Ios, la chiquita

con los ferries de mayo
ios empieza a mover las aspas
y restregarse los ojos,

a ratos veneciana
a ratos ortodoxa
casi siempre discoteca

como ningún dios del olimpo
o siquiera un héroe despistado
anduvo haciendo travesuras por aquí
escasos de tragedias
tuvimos que conformarnos con un incierto certificado
de nacimiento o defunción
de mamá homero
y aunque parezca mentira
nadie más

encalarlo todo es la consigna
para que los jóvenes forunculosos del atlántico norte
aprendan a mear desde las azoteas

tetradracmas o euros
con que pagar el éxtasis
tienen por efigie la diosa con ojos de mochuelo

para seguir en argumento
nada como el recuerdo de lo invisible

Ios, the Little One

with the ferries of May
Ios begins to crank up her blades
and rub her eyes

at times Venetian
at others Orthodox
nearly always disco

as no other god from Olympus
or even a hero lost on his way
got up to any mischief around here
scarcely any tragedy
we had to make do with the tentative
birth or death certificate
of Homer's mother
and no one else
believe it or not

whitewashing everything is the order of the day
so that the furunculous youths from the North Atlantic
learn to piss from the rooftops

Tetra-drachmas or Euros
with which to buy ecstasy
bear the effigy of the goddess with owl's eyes

there's nothing like the memory of the invisible
to continue along this storyline

Érase Belle Isle

1

la isla abraza
caben y valen
pasos
borregos
avutardas
faisanes
la línea de horizonte más perfecta
el nombre de los vientos
y los mástiles

además de
arena
fulgores
herrumbre
mi dependencia
de la vida, el cayado
las ortigas

y un banco cualquiera de plaza
frente al mar
pero no vuelvas
la cabeza aunque te llamen el ave fénix
el pájaro roc
la sirena
la esmeralda puroamor

Once upon Belle Isle

1

the island embraces
pathways
yearling sheep
great bustards
pheasants
all have their place thereon
the most perfect horizon
the name of the winds
and masts

as well as
sand
glows
rust
my dependence on
life, a crook
nettles

and any old bench
looking out over the sea
but don't look
round even if you're called by the phoenix
the rukh
the mermaid
the emerald purelove

2

el profesor de esquí valenciano
cuenta sus años en Laponia
cuando la noche boreal
los mosquitos carniceros
la gente que trasiega con ramos de abedul
flagelándose
ahuyentando
nada

es Semana Santa
en el mundo
de gigantes y cabezudos
y peregrinos como tábanos

el vino blanco
seco
con sabor a uva pasa
en copa grácil y mesa de caoba antigua
con la alta marea
a medianoche de plenilunio
excele

2

the ski instructor from Valencia
tells of his years in Lapland
the arctic night
flesh-eating mosquitos
people who shuffle around with birch-wood branches
self-flagellating
banishing
nothing

it's Easter
in the world
of giants and those with bulbous heads
and pilgrims like horseflies

the dry
white wine
with the taste of raisin
in a slender glass and an antique mahogany table
high tide
at midnight under a full moon
in excelsis

3

la mujer del albañil padece esclerosis
cada vez que la cruzo
zancudo
el mal avanza

el ebanista goza la herencia mal habida
de alguien a quien dispensó un oportuno perdigón
los hijos se le suicidaron
y atormentan al pueblo
cuando graznan los albatros del anochecer

3

The stonemason's wife suffers from sclerosis
each time our paths cross
the sickness advances
on stilts

the cabinetmaker enjoys his dubiously acquired inheritance
from someone to whom he dispensed an opportune bullet
his children committed suicide on him
and torment the town
when the albatrosses squawk at nightfall

4

el alma se complace en las islas
las alacenas son fragantes
las puertas y labios muy labrados
casi no existen cercas, barreras
ni cerrojos
para pescar sombras
mejor promesas y canciones
que los anzuelos, las boyas
los arpones
esta red

4

the soul takes pleasure on the islands
the pantries are fragrant
the doors and their frames are intricately carved
walls, gates
or bolts are scarce
better a promise or a song
to catch shadows
than fishhooks, buoys
harpoons
this net

Cielito lindo

a Lik

Anacrónico
El sol
En las mariposas
Invernales
En el aroma
Inefable de las fresias

Humedad porteña
                    gris
A más no poder
casas bajas, rejas en las ventanas, plantas floridas
las comunardas, de toda la vida,
                felicidad del hogar.

Los hombres anuncios
de empanadas, vinos o colchones
Bailan patéticos en los cruces de avenidas
rieles zigzagueantes de la vida
pero
una humillación más
qué le hace al tigre

Cielito Lindo [1]

to Lik

Anachronic
The sun
In the winter
Butterflies
In the ineffable aroma
Of the freesias

Porteño[2] humidity
                    grey
to the utmost extreme
low-rise houses, bars on the windows, plants in flower
            busy lizzies
                    lifelong communards

Human billboards advertising
pasties, wines or mattresses
Dance pathetically at the crossroads of avenues
part of life's rich tapestry
but
just another brick
in the wall

---

[1] "Cielito lindo" [Pretty little darling] is the title of a popular Mexican song, usually played by a mariachi band.
[2] Native to or inhabitant of Buenos Aires.

Ritos de escritura y concentración
Levantarse tarde o temprano, té, café, caminar, en un lugar suntuoso
en un cuadernito con lápiz que destiñe.
Descifrar la intimidad
indescifrable.
El amor, asimétrico por naturaleza
entra en la categoría
de gran desaire

El poema
Un cuerpo
El país

así es la escritura

Rituals of writing and concentration
Get up late or early, tea, coffee, wandering
in a sumptuous place
in a notebook with pencil that fades.
Decipher undecipherable
intimacy.
Love, lopsided by nature
enters into the category
of utmost disdain

The poem
A body
The homeland

that's what writing is about

Después del 11 de setiembre el 11 de marzo, el julio de londres
el miedo a lo lovecraft es difuso,
hasta que aparecieron manchitas, subproductos locales
miedos circunscritos; al ántrax, a la bomba sucia, a los de mirada
aviesa en los aviones, miedo al futuro.
Variaciones tenaces del mismo miedo.

After 11th September comes 11th March, July in London
fear at large Lovecraft-style,
until blemishes appeared, local by-products
circumscribed fears: of anthrax, the dirty bomb, of those with a malevolent
sideways glance at airplanes, fear of the future.
Tenacious variations on the same fear.

Cada poema cada novela
es una guía centrada en algo común a otros
percibida del ángulo del relator
Ese mínimo común denominador hace que uno pueda
entrar, comulgar
disputarse con el escritor, retarlo a duelo, correr
a campo traviesa
a veces mano tendida
otra linterna de diógenes en el firmamento

Each poem each novel
is a guide centred on something common to others
perceived from the angle of the narrator
This minimum common denominator means that one can
enter, share
argue with the writer, throw things back in her face, run
cross country
sometimes hand held out
another Diogenesian lantern in the firmament

Recomponer las sonatinas de clementi
en las yemas encallecidas de cuando quinceañeras
en los ojos fatigados
la retama refulgente de bonnard
el bosque irredento de bacon
los pliegues, los trazos, los pozos
cierta luz fosforescente
tanto desorden
y harta calderilla

La taracea es una técnica artesanal que consiste en incrustar
materiales diversos en los muebles
sin esfuerzo aparente

Cielo cielito lindo cielito alto. Diáfano.
Celeste proclama, celeste bandera de escuela primaria.

Un ombú derramado, sin contención, más allá de la frontera
de la propia idea ombú.
Plaza Francia.
Luz de julio.

Recompose Clementi's sonatinas
in the calloused fingertips of when we were fifteen years old
in our exhausted eyes
the resplendent broom of Bonnard
Bacon's inveterate forest
the folds, brushstrokes, wells
certain phosphorescent light
so much disarray
and a load of loose change

Marquetry is an artisanal technique in ornamentation which consists of
    inlaying
various materials into a piece of furniture
without apparent force

Cielo, cielito lindo cielito alto. Crystal-clear.
Celestial proclamation, sky-blue flag at primary school.

An ombu tree, spilt without containment, beyond the frontier
of the very idea of an ombu
Plaza Francia.[1]
Light of July.

---

[1] A square-cum-park in the Recoleta neighbourhood of Buenos Aires—a popular place of encounter, particularly at the weekends.

Claves: 130, 29, 60, 108, 267.
Los colectivos atraviesan plazuchas ralas para hacerte presente
que en tu vida
no te quepa duda
arrecia invierno.

Vivir en los márgenes
es un lugar como cualquier otro.
Lugar de las palabras entre las grietas.

El desierto, ¿crece o florece?
El desierto, olvido del árbol.

Codes: 130, 29, 60, 108, 267.
Buses cut across sparse little old squares to remind yourself
that in life
there is no room for doubt
winter worsens.

Living on the margins
is a place like any other.
Place of words in the crevices.

The desert, does it grow or flower?
The desert, oblivion of the tree.

Parque de Barrancas:

la baranda desvencijada, las estatuas chapuceramente pintadas de negro tienen un cerco con candado imponente que cuida próceres desconocidos. Uno, por razón ignota, tiene su nombre en cirílico. La placa lo pregona en 1837 apóstol de la libertad búlgara. Su apellido es Vasilevsky.

Héroe desconocido, adiós

Un perímetro sórdido para perros, la calvicie del infierno tiene que ser así. Paseadores, correas, detritos. Tráficos. Pesadilla. Tengo la boca reseca de fantasmas. Los de plena luz y carne y sangre. Los peores.

Los crepusculares se llaman cartoneros y destripan los hedores materiales del inconsciente ciudadano y Buenos Aires es una tiznada, afanosa Villa Miseria de Calcuta.

O no, porque enfrente un restaurante diz que elegante se llama SALVAME MARIA.

En 1480 Ercole de Roberti pintó

Los argonautas abandonan Cólquida. Y saludan mirando el río.

Confusión de presagios y pañuelos. ¿Los blancos para el luto?

¿Los negros para las ceremonias de rigor?

deme dos

Deme Dos.

Parque de Barrancas: [1]

the ramshackle railings, the statues slapdashedly painted black have a fence with an imposing padlock that guards unknown heroes. One, for some unknown reason, bears his name in Cyrillic. The plaque proclaims him in 1837 an apostle of Bulgarian liberty. His surname is Vasilevsky.

Goodbye, unknown hero.

A sordid perimeter for dogs, hell's baldness has to be like that. Dog walkers, leashes, litter. Traffic. Nightmare. My mouth is shrivelled up with ghosts. Those of broad daylight and flesh and blood. The worst.

Those who come out at dusk are called *cartoneros*[2] and strip the malodorous materials of the oblivious citizen and Buenos Aires becomes a wretched, teeming shanty town of Calcutta.

Or not, because opposite a supposedly elegant restaurant is called SAVE ME MARY

In 1480 Ercole de Roberti painted

The Argonauts leaving Colchis. And they wave looking at the river.

A muddle of omens and scarves. The white ones for mourning?

The black ones for customary ceremonies?

just give me two

Just Give Me Two.

---

[1] A well-known park in the Belgrano neighbourhood of Buenos Aires.
[2] A *cartonero* is a waste picker who recovers recyclable material thrown out by others in order to sell it on.

CRÓNICAS

CHRONICLES

Cuarteto de Praga

hotel mucha, calle sokolovská, praga

primer piso, enfrente, una llamita,
la ventana, a medio tapar por papeles de diario
qué ilumina?
alguien la mueve
es viernes santo
el viento arrecia
nieva sobre los callejones del prestigio
malá strana
casi nombre y apellido de tango

tranvías repletos de gente bien sombría

Prague Quartet

Hotel Mucha, Sokolovská Street, Prague

first floor, door opposite, a little flame
the window, half covered with newspaper
what's it illuminating?
someone moves it
it's Good Friday
the wind picks up
snow on the alleys of the prestigious
Malá Strana
almost the name and surname of a tango

trams chock-full of cheerless passengers

2

praga es
–además
de turistas de provincias–
un idioma sin gente amable
será por el viento,
porque no tienen vocales

una foto de gauguin en casa de mucha
en calzoncillos, tocando el piano
parece un foxtrot

milagro de sobrevivencia
mercerías, vitrinas a la qué me importa,
tiendas de los años cincuenta

gilda que no para de agonizar en la misma bolsa de arpillera
el duque, nosotros
las estatuas de los puentes
tiritamos
y piafamos

2

Prague is
—aside
from tourists from the provinces—
a language without kindly people
it must be because of the wind
because they have no vowels

a photo of Gauguin
in briefs, playing
what seems to be a foxtrot
on the piano
in Mucha's house

the miracle of survival
haberdashery, shop windows displaying whatever,
shops from the nineteen fifties

Gilda caught inescapably in death throes in the same bag made of
        sack cloth
the Duke, we
the statues on the bridges
shiver
and stamp the ground

diálogo en la taberna de cerveza negra
con pareja navarra dueños de una ferretería
fueron de excursión a terezín (!), arantxa insiste
la verdad que el sitio no es bonito
no es bonito el sitio…
josema, para congraciarse conmigo, cuenta
cuánto más amables somos nos, los argentinos
él nos conoce bien porque va a matar palomas a la provincia de córdoba
aunque siempre tiene problemas para llevar y traer las escopetas
digo, en su córdoba *lejana y sola* no hay torcazas que se presten
a ser asesinadas por mi contratista de pamplona?

las torcazas argentinas tenemos –claro está–
reputación de ser más querendonas

conversation in the tavern that serves stout
with a couple from Navarra, owners of an ironmonger's
they went on an excursion to Terezín (!), Arantxa insists
the place really isn't pretty
not pretty at all…
in order to ingratiate himself with me, Josema tells me
how much friendlier we, the Argentineans, are
he knows us because he goes pigeon shooting in the province of Córdoba
although he always has problems getting his rifles there and back
I mean, in his own native Córdoba, *distant and alone*, are there no doves
      who volunteer
to be assassinated by my contractor from Pamplona?

we Argentine doves—there it is—have
a reputation for being affectionate

3

de pronto
un tufo
de aguas servidas
fermentadas
de venceslao muerto a manos
de su hermano boleslao hace la friolera de 1800 años

en italiano dicen
simplemente
la fogna

hordas de sedientos
de molduras doradas se abaten
sobre praga que alguna vez fue esquiva
y ahora vende kipás de plástico por cinco coronas
y hand made golem
en arcilla en mazapán
y tickets uno a uno
paso a paso

vanidad de las cortezas
los fulgores
hasta las cenizas

3

a stench
of fermented
raw sewage
of Wenceslas dead at the hands
of his brother Boleslav a mere 1800 years ago

in Italian they
simply say
la fogna

hoards of those who're hungry
for gilded moulding swoop down
on a Prague that was once avoided
and now sells plastic kippahs for five crowns
and handmade Golem
out of clay and marzipan
and tickets one by one
step by step

vanity of the tree bark
the glows
even the cinders

claro que había oído   visto   sufrido
los dibujos de los chicos de terezín
"aquí no vi mariposas"
"tiene que existir un mundo donde no haya sino patatas negras"
sin embargo veros detrás de una vitrina
es otro cantar
chicos chicos de todos los dolores
aquí morimos y alcanzan los dedos de las manos
a los seis
siete ocho nueve añitos
un día como hoy
los turistas desfilamos ante ustedes
arracimados partiendo de la foto con rodete
de la maestra *brandeis*
y la valija de cartón

entre VOSOTROS y nosotros
una cortina de vidrio y lágrimas
que jamás enjugarán

of course I had seen   heard   suffered
the drawings by the children of Terezín
"I didn't see butterflies here"
"must there exist a world in which there are nothing but black potatoes"
to see you behind a shop window is nevertheless
another song
children, children of all the agonies
here we die and the tips of our fingers reach out to
the six
seven- eight- nine-year-olds
on a day like today
we, the tourists parade before you
clustered together as we leave the photo
of the teacher *Brandeis* [1] with her hair tied up in a bun
and the cardboard suitcase

a curtain of glass and tears
between YOU and us
that can never be wiped away

---

[1] (The artist Friedl Dicker Brandeis (Vienna 1898–Auschwitz 1944) set up clandestine drawing and painting workshops for children in the Terezín concentration camp. Before her deportation to Auschwitz, in October 1944, Friedl packed some 5,000 drawings done by her students into two suitcases which she then hid. They were discovered ten years later.)

bajo el mismo cielo
las lápidas
torcidas por vientos desdichados
el pobre rabino de praga
nunca pudo dar paz a sus huesos
tanto lo atosigamos de deseos genéricos, volátiles
que no retienen las estelas
de piedritas ni papel impreso
paz
    dicha
        salud
el golem jamás fue creado para mitigar pesares
sino para barrer los patios de escombros y plegarias
incumplidas

underneath the same sky
the gravestones
left crooked by the wretched winds
the poor Rabbi of Prague
his bones could never rest in peace
so much did we badger him with volatile, generic wishes
that neither the trails of little pebbles
nor printed paper retain
peace
       happiness
              health
the Golem was never created to alleviate sorrows
but to sweep patios clean of rubble and unfulfilled
entreaties

en español, en el baño de mujeres, coronas diez del cementerio:
hacer negocio de una tragedia es morir viviendo
¡abajo las religiones
viva la libertad!
sigue firma compuesta por dos acentos circunflejos

los comentarios y advertencias del golem
suelen ser tan pertinentes
que los comerciantes apresurados los friegan y borran
con lejía de sangre y huesos al amanecer

una golondrina sin verano tirita
atrapada por las rejas del desconsuelo

written in Spanish, in the Ladies at the cemetery, for a fee of ten crowns:
hacer negocio de una tragedia es morir viviendo
¡abajo las religiones
viva la libertad!
                  [making business out of a tragedy is a living death
                  down with religion
                  long live freedom!]
a signature composed of two circumflex accents follows

the comments and warnings of the Golem
are usually so pertinent
that hurried traders scour to erase them
with the lye of blood and bones at dawn

one swallow, shivering trapped behind the bars of grief
does not a summer make

4

apiñados, en hileras con idénticos rompevientos de colores
los veraneantes mezclan confundidos
el miércoles agrio, el jueves santo, la pascua florida y la de resurrección
pagan con alineada paciencia
en las ruletas que florecen con sus máquinas vocingleras a cada esquina
en la catedral de san vito –donde si quieres orar sinceramente puedes
hacerlo gratis entre ocho y media y nueve en punto de la mañana

en el casi desierto museo de sagaces vigilantes
los bassano, tintoretto, rembrandt,
greco y durero me piden que les de un poco de mi savia para nutrirles
      con mis avideces
y los acaricio
intercambiamos santo y seña, estigmas
por los siglos de los siglos
amén

Volver al remitente:

Gregorio Samsa ya no vive aquí
Ni yo tampoco.

abril 08

4

jammed tightly into rows with identical colourful windcheaters
the summer holidaymakers confusedly mix up
Holy Wednesday, Maundy Thursday, Easter of the Feast of Flowers and
    that of the Resurrection
they pay with regimented patience
for the roulettes that emerge on every street corner with their garrulous
    machines
in Saint Vitus Cathedral—between eight thirty and nine o'clock sharp
you can pray for free if you sincerely
wish to do so

in the almost deserted museum of sagacious guards
the works of Bassano, Tintoretto, Rembrandt,
El Greco and Dürer ask that I bequeath them a little of my sap to nourish
    them with my avidity
and I caress them
we exchange shibboleths, stigmas
unto the ages of ages
amen

Return to sender:

Gregor Samsa no longer lives here.
And neither do I.

April '08

Ortigas de saorge

frente a mi celda, montaña soleada
bajo la torre que da al claustro
un cuadrante solar
donde quedó escrito
a me il sole a te lo studio
enigma a resolver
quién es **me**
quién **te**
una interpretación razonable pretende
que el hablante sería el cuadrante
amonestando a los hermanos
ser prudentes con el tiempo

en el corredor
para quien levante la vista un medallón
feo, desangelado
en ornadas letras azul, verde y beige
MODESTIA

Nettles from Saorge

In front of my cell, mountain bathed in sunshine
under the tower which leads to the cloisters
a sundial
where it remains written
a me il sole a te lo studio
riddle to be solved
who is **me**
who is **te**
one reasonable interpretation claims
that the speaker might be the sundial
admonishing its brothers
to be prudent with time

in the hallway
for whoever looks up
an ugly, charmless medallion
in ornate blue, green and beige letters
MODESTY

cuesta empinada
tomar resuello en una casa con pegatina
free tibet

sestear para gente y para ganado
es verbo

sarta de náufragos
girando entre las aspas
de un improbable molino

steep slope
catching one's breath in a house bearing the sticker
free Tibet

to siesta for people and cattle
is a verb

string of shipwrecks
spinning around in between the blades
of an unlikely windmill

la jardinera cuenta que se brotó en china en un congreso de neurocirugía, tiene un discurso apasionado sobre la imposibilidad del pequeño cultivador de fabricar abono con pienso de ortigas, cuestión que incluso se debate en el parlamento europeo. cae de inmediato en un atareado rigor de tareas que nunca concluirá hasta que una noche a la hora del lobo una lengua de bruma la disipó.
    otra comensal se ocupa de un hogar para sobrevivientes de auschwitz
quienes le dejaron en prenda su mirar huidizo y apaleado
el marido, maoísta confeso, termina de profesor especializado
en falsos amigos y trampas de la traducción.
comparto con ellos
la última cucharada de este caldo de ortigas
confeccionado por los cuidados de la maligna
melusina de lusignan
por ella primavera es falsa
y nieva a más no poder

the gardener recounts that she suffered a breakdown in China at a congress on neurosurgery, she gives an impassioned speech about the inability of small farmers to make compost out of feed made from nettles, an issue which is even being debated in the European Parliament, and she falls immediately into an overwhelming, strict set of endless tasks until one night at the hour of the wolf a swathe of fog swallows her up.

    another guest looks after a home for survivors of Auschwitz
to whom they pledged their startled and paled looks
her husband, a self-confessed Maoist, ends up as a professor
              specialising
in false friends and traps of translation
I share with them
the last spoonful of nettle soup
brewed under the cares of the malignant
Melusine de Lusignan
because of her spring is fake
and it snows to her heart's content

me rozo con fabuladoras, pavorreales
del yo sin fondo y la voz ingrata
alguna triste parejas de cotorras
con la cresta desplumada
inseparables
y otra relumbrante como
bálsamo de meridión

en este lugar escarpado
hay desfile carnestolendo
una rubia urticante me cuestiona por el empleo de la ducha
de la única computadora me cuestionaría a dentelladas sobre todo, creo
en el único bar verdulería
una londinense relata que vino con su marino sueco que buscaba una
        montaña
vista en sueños y la encontró aquí
ahora ambos viven de changas, ella en el geriátrico
él de albañil
un italiano de arles exige que por las mañanas le abran la sacristía
para cantar porque sin higiene para sus cuerdas vocales
no puede vivir
al día siguiente huye
abandonando en su retirada fideos bio y un par de dientes de ajo
prefirió desentonar bajo las aguas más benévolas
de la llanura del Po

I rub shoulders with storytellers, peacocks
of a thankless voice and bottomless ego
some sad inseparable
pair of parrots
with plucked crests
and another resplendent like
meridian balm

in this steep place
there's a carnival parade
a stinging blond bites me with questions about my light and my shadow
the number of brown dwarfs in the sky
and how many pieces of toast are allowed per head during the coffee break
in the only greengrocer's
a Londoner tells of how she came with her Swedish sailor who was looking
    for a mountain
seen in his dreams and he found it here
now both make a living doing odd jobs, she in the retirement home
he as a bricklayer
a southerner from Arles requests that the sacristy be opened for him each
    morning
so that he can sing because without cleanliness of the vocal cords
one cannot live
the following day he flees
relinquishing in his retreat organic noodles and a couple of garlic cloves
left under his pillow to ward off the vampires
he preferred to sing his excess out of tune
under the most benevolent waters
of the Po Valley

un caminante tuerto estrafalario
otro haciendo eses que me inspira resquemor
un grupo con palos practica algún tipo de arte marcial dizque oriental
en la plaza es domingo
pero no de ramos

sueño con anacondas
jaurías contra natura
en mi propio cuarto
llamo a madre pero estoy áfona
no me acuerdo para nada la calle, de paso,
en la que vivo
decía
digo

un plato regional que no sé en qué consiste
se llama *merda di can*
literal
averiguo
son inocentes ñoquis verdes que parecen caseros
otro es la *socca*, hermana melliza
cosas que uno se entera, de la porteña fainá

an eccentric one-eyed walker
another staggering along who stirs up resentment in me
a group with poles practices some kind of seemingly oriental martial art
in the square it's Sunday
but not of palms

I dream about anacondas
aberrant hounds
in my bedroom
I call out for mother but I'm without voice
I do not, by the way, remember the street
in which I live
at all
I used to say
I still say

a regional dish which consists of I-don't-know-what
is called *merda di can* [1]
literally?
I find out
innocent green gnocchis that appear homemade
another is the *socca*, their twin sister
things that one learns, from the *porteña fainá* [2]

---

[1] *Merda di can* refers to Niçois gnocchis made with Swiss chard. Here, the author plays with the double meaning, as *merda di can* also evokes the idea of "dog shit".
[2] *Porteño fainá* refers to a savory tart made from chickpeas that is typical to Buenos Aires.

nos visita hortense para que admiremos sus logros comarcales
la resurrección de la cofradía de los penitentes blancos
con subsidio estatal y autorización de procesión
para erradicar del pueblo todo tipo de embriaguez
la fe le permite multiplicar el tiempo entre sus manos
seis hijos, visitar a los ancianos
y llevar a bien un próspero salón de té

y pensar que cuando digo
escribo
esta gente
está incluída
hormiguean sus cuitas en una escalera de caracol que desciende hasta la
        ciénaga
y asciende lóbrega a ninguna parte
que yo sepa

al salir la calle se llama
repentia
no hay otra
que arrepentirse
por hazañas y por sañas
por ferocidad y la mi tanta mansedumbre

Hortense pays us a visit so that we can admire his local achievements
resurrection of the fraternity of the penitent white men
with a state subsidy and permission to go in procession
to eradicate all states of drunkenness from the town
faith enables him to multiply time within his hands
six children, to visit the elderly
and successfully run a prosperous tea shop

and to think that when I say
I write
these people
are included
their worries swarm up and down a spiral staircase that leads down to the
        swamp
and drearily goes up to nowhere
as far as I know

upon going out the street is called
repentia
there's nothing else left to do
but to regret
valiant escapades and cruelty
ferocity and my great meekness

la montaña alpina labró gestas en escritura cuneiforme
para mi asombro
como antes tejió quipus para abrigarme el desamparo
nevado, el illimani cerca de la paz
pero a menos que uno les imponga las manos las piedras no laten

en santa cruz tapizaban mi memoria
huesos de mango, en beth shearim
olivos nudosos aquí, en saorge también

sigo pensando que los bordes
y márgenes
evidenciamos las dolencias
que oscurecen el centro.
la noche sigue inmensa estrellada
y la mañana fulgura de retamas
recibí
hace mucho que me despido
mi urticante
soledad

the alpine mountain tilled heroic deeds in cuneiform writing
to my astonishment
as before it wove *quipus* [1] to shelter my helplessness
the snow-covered Illimani close to La Paz
but the rocks only palpitate when one performs the laying on of hands

in Santa Cruz mango bones
upholstered my memory, gnarled olive trees
in Beth She'arim, here too in Saorge

I keep thinking that we the edges
and margins
demonstrate the ailments
that darken the centre.
the night continues to be thick
starlit
and the morning aglow with broom
I said goodbye a long time ago
please welcome
my stinging
solitude

---

[1] *Quipus* are composed of a series of cords, which were used by the Inca community to record information about society by means of encoded knots in the cords.

Gambier, Ohio

El *Columbus Dispatch* en primera página publica que uno de cada cuatro linyeras del país, son veteranos de guerra. De ellos, medio millón -en algún período-, no tuvo techo.
Primero la guerra, después la calle.

L'América profunda es opulenta
y empecinada
mezcla no siempre feliz de águila, bisonte
elefante y oso de circo,
(dizque) domesticados

push pull sale off
compulsivas
las palabras los enseres las frutas y las máquinas

muestras bien ritmadas de afecto calendario
regifting
refilling

Gambier, Ohio

The *Columbus Dispatch* runs on its front page that one in four of the country's casual labourers are war veterans. Of them, half a million have—at some point—not had a roof over their heads.

First war, then the street.

Deep America is opulent
and hard-headed
not always a happy mix of (ostensibly) domesticated
eagle, bison,
elephant and circus bear

push pull sale off
compulsive
words tools fruit and machines

displays of affection well-regimented by the calendar
regifting
refilling

Los padres de los chicos pagan aquí 50.000 dólares para graduarse en temas singulares y luego errar de becarios por el mundo mansa, prolijamente entre los pobres para quedárselos para siempre en el alhajero del corazón

–Visité su país a los 17. Su acento hasta me conmueve.

Me devolvía a mi hotel y pasamos media hora en alguna ruta, alguna noche. Debió ser por Gambier, Ohio. Sharon dice que a su marido tras quince años de entusiasmo por las finanzas de la universidad lo rescindieron.

Una vez conversó cinco minutos en pijama, recalca la pronunciación, bien abierta, *pa-ya-ma*, con Paul Newman y hablaron de sus respectivos perros. El de ella o el de él habían escapado. Paul es muy generoso y cada tanto da uno que otro seminario de teatro en forma gratuita. También me relató que la pelambre de su *Lorraine* es color ámbar, mejor dicho miel de montaña.

Here, parents pay 50,000 dollars for their children to graduate in any old subject and then roam meekly and impeccably turned out with a scholarship around the world amidst the poor to treasure them forever in the heart

—I visited your country at the age of 17. Your accent touches even me.

She dropped me off at my hotel and we spent half an hour on some road, one night. It must've been somewhere around Gambier, Ohio. Sharon says of her husband that after fifteen years as an enthusiastic employee of the university treasury, they kicked him out.

She once chatted to Paul Newman for five minutes in her pajamas. She stresses the pronunciation, mouth wide open, *pa-ja-mas*. They spoke about their respective dogs. Either his or hers had escaped. Paul is most generous and every now and again gives the odd seminar on theatre for free. She also told me that the fleece of her *Lorraine* is amber-colored, or rather mountain honey.

Xenofobia vegetal : los *Russian olives* fueron decretados plaga estadual y sólo en un trecho del camino talarán, más de 1.500 porque les comen el pan y el agua a otros honestos árboles y matorrales oriundos del lugar.
Parecen acebos y los pájaros les picotean los frutitos amarillos.
En español les decimos paraíso. La hoja, no me lo invento
se llama **angustifolia**.

Encaje, babita del diablo
la nieve
frágil
    brillante
        tan luminosa
que obliga a rezar por dentro

Viajando se conoce gente

Vegetable xenophobia : *Russian olives* have been decreed a state plague and just on one stretch of road they will chop down more than 1,500 because they eat the bread and water of other innocent trees and brushwood native to the area.

They look like holly and the birds peck at their yellow fruit.

In Spanish we call them paradise. The leaf, I'm not making it up is called **angustifolia**.

Lace, dew drops of the Devil's drool
snow
fragile
    brilliant
        so luminescent
that it forces one to pray inside

When travelling one meets people

Hoy, jueves, toca recoger hojas de plátano en grandes lonas de plástico azul

–Es un trabajo infinito, los vecinos no lo hacen, el viento me trae las de todos–

–Soy directora del museo Tepapa

–Los años impares hago con dos amigos el camino de Santiago entre 20 y 30 km diarios

–Cubano sí, gusano no. Me presento. Cuando me preguntan, Alcibíades, ¿por qué vives aquí?, digo: porque se me da la gana.

Saskia hizo, a mi pedido, una fotocopia del árbol de la vida. Me mostró
el punto LUCA
Last Unknown Common Ancestor
grado cero de la vida
grado cero del poema
una y otro en perpetua construcción

Today, Thursday, it's time to gather plane leaves up in large blue plastic tarpaulins
—It's an endless task, my neighbours don't do it, the wind brings everyone else's over to me
—I'm Director of the Tepapa Museum
—On odd-numbered years I do in between 20 and 30 kms a day along St. James' Way with a couple of friends
—Cuban yes, *gusano*[1] no. Let me introduce myself. When they ask me: Alcibiades, why do you live here? I say: because I feel like it.

At my request, Saskia made a photocopy of the tree of life. She showed me
The LUCA point
Last Unknown Common Ancestor
zero degrees of life
zero degrees of the poem
both in perpetual construction

---

[1] *Gusano* is the name given by Fidel Castro to Cuban exiles to the United States after the Cuban revolution. He considered them to be bourgeois counter-revolutionaries and no loss to Cuba, hence the term *gusano* [worm].

Términos: Padres, madres, profesores se prospectan
        Los estudiantes en cambio se cautivan y seducen
A veces se cazan y mueren como bambis
Uno se desnucó en el baño
Otro quedó rígido, aterido en el gimnasio borrachito
quién sabe de amor
Pobres ciervitos, carnes de cañón

En el cementerio, fotografío un finadito con lápida ilegible del siglo pasado
y banderita reciente de la Unión

El pasado, ¿es lo de menos o lo de más?
La nieve puso relativo punto final a la hojarasca

Los campus, nudo gordiano de estas aglomeraciones en medio
de ninguna parte y pura desesperanza
uno que otro pájaro mecánico de pico corvo y movimiento perpetuo
extrae fósiles a la pradera pajiza
que se deja

Carreteras con la raya partida al medio.
Idénticas marcas, idénticas ofertas
acumulo, apilo, luego existo

Terms: Fathers, mothers, teachers survey
     Students in contrast captivate and seduce one another
Sometimes they hunt one another and die like Bambis
One broke her neck in the bath
Another ended up rigid, frozen stiff legless in the gymnasium
Who knows about love
Poor deer or gazelles, sitting ducks

In the cemetery, I photograph a deceased man with an illegible headstone
     from the last century
bearing the recent Union Flag

The past: is it the least or the most of our worries?
The snow puts a relative end to the carpet of dead leaves

The campuses, Gordian knot of these agglomerations in the middle
of nowhere and pure grief
the odd mechanical bird with a hooked beak in continuous movement
extracts fossils from the straw meadow
which allows it to

Highways with a dividing line down the middle
Identical brands, identical offers
I accumulate, pile up, therefore I exist

irredentos viejitos
bien situados
cebados de falsa mansedumbre y verdadero aburrimiento
en el armario mal que bien oculto tras los abrigos
una que otra escopeta
al alcance de la mano
conservan los pecados capitales en vistosas cápsulas floridas
píldoras de día, pildoras de noche y de entrepierna
prótesis crepusculares
regulan los humores, la avaricia, la gula,
el fluir de las arterias, sexo y seso
esperanza
no

unrepentant well situated
little old men
loaded with false docility and true boredom
in the wardrobe somehow or other hidden behind the overcoats
the odd shotgun or two
within arm's reach
they preserve mortal sin in attractive florid capsules
pills for the day, pills for the night and those for between the legs
twilight prosthesis
regulate mood swings, greed, gluttony,
the flow of the arteries, genitals and brain
hope
no

en verano se precipitan diez días a las costas *me-mé*
mediterráneas o mexicanas
para buscar el santo grial, la eterna juventud
y una que otra convención
congreso coloquio que facilite al menos una discreta polución nocturna,
esmerile o alargue unos centímetros
el pene o el *cv*

en tierra de ciegos el insomnio es rey

jibarizar berlín, gambier o davenport
granada, bari o poitiers
jibarizar, repito
es la consigna

in the summer ten days fly by on the *me-me*
Mediterranean or Mexican coasts
to search for the Holy Grail, eternal youth
and a convention
congress, colloquium or two which facilitate at least one discreet nocturnal
fling, it polishes or lengthens by a few centimetres
the penis or the *cv*

in a land of the blind the insomniac is king

shrink Berlin, Gambier or Davenport
Granada, Bari or Poitiers
Shrink, I repeat
is the order

los rituales del insomnio son singulares
repaso así cuanto supe de las ceremonias malagán, Papúa, tallados de urdimbres inextricables para los muertos, para pagar deudas y dirimir disputas.
no me bastan y voy
al libro de cuáquero en cuerina azul
cajón derecho en la mesita de luz
–génesis 6–4–
la página me arroja los *nefilim*,
que son los ángeles gigantes
cayeron sobre nosotros y se fueron
a vivir en cuevas altísimas de improbables respiraderos
circulares

la cama es descomunal
duermo poco y enrevesado

zona ácida del sueño, neblina de los instintos, ceguera de las
    emociones
consternación y ceniza
bronca diamantina,
jabón negro sin embargo limpia, disuelve
papel de lija mejor

the rituals of insomnia are peculiar

this is how I go over how much I knew about the Malagan ceremonies, Papua, sculpted by intricate warps for the dead, to pay debts and settle disputes

not enough for me and I go

to the Quaker book of wisdom with a blue leather cover

right hand draw in the bedside locker

—**Genesis 6-4**—

the page tosses the Nephilim

who are giant angels

at me

they fell down on us and went

to live in high caves of improbable

circular vents

the bed is colossal

I sleep very little, am restless

acid zone of sleep, fog of instincts, blindness of emotions

consternation and ash

adamantine fury,

black soap nevertheless cleanses, dissolves

sandpaper better still

el sueño, si llega, tiene cosas singulares
los muertos trabajan sin cambiar un ápice:
berta bajaba anoche para cobrarme seis noches de hotel
en venecia alguien, muy elegante, como la signorina *elettra* de
donna leon, qué hacía?

–conocí una así cuando yo tenía 22 y trabajaba en orbital publicidad con carlos muerto relativamente reciente, a él le gustaba ella más que yo, en realidad no se llamaba electra sino eleonora y berta murió sin querer ni creer en mis letras y carlos ignorando en mí el hijo que nunca nos nació

sleep, if indeed it arrives, throws up odd things
the dead work without changing a thing:
Berta came down last night to charge me for six nights at the hotel in Venice, someone very elegant like Signorina *Electra* of *Donna Leon*, what was she doing?

—I met someone like that when I was 22 and worked at orbital advertising with Carlos who passed away recently, he liked her more than me, in truth she wasn't called Electra but Eleonora and Berta died without loving or believing in my writing and Carlos unaware of the child I bore, ours who was never born

les digo
bájense del bronce, tiriten
que un resto de *vendetta* perenne los nombra
con dolor y mi parte angélica de *nefilá* que rodó
os condena desde mi abovedado tragaluz
a lentísimo purgatorio como lo que son
meros
méritos
subrayo
enanos de jardín

la vejez es un trabajo a tiempo completo
un trabajo de esclavos

I say to you all
get down off your pedestals, confront the cold
let the leftovers of perennial *vendetta* name you
with pain and my angelic side from Nephila that fell
condemn you from my vaulted skylight
to slow purgatory as you are
I emphasize
mere
measly little
garden gnomes

old age is a full time job
the work of slaves

en la biblioteca nacional asistí a una expo
también ella trashumante
llamada *infierno* cuyo fondo está constituido por textos e imágenes de obras censuradas
en este texto qué tijereteo qué pudre en el placard
un par de abuelos a veces biliosos otras zalameros que cargan, sin que a primera vista les pese expedientes varios por desfalcos y acosos a menores y mayores, un par de amigos de los que me alejo definitivamente que defienden a ultranza que coger niños es un índice extremo de cariño que los griegos y que foucault, gide y blablablá
una que otra zancadilla de normal administración
ni el college ni las orgas hacen mayores olas, prestigio obliga
y los mandan de vuelta a casa circulen que no hay nada que ver,
hagan juego
señores no va más
negro el cero

I visited an exhibition at the national library
also roving
called *inferno* the content of which is composed of texts and images
from censored works
in this text that I snip
what skeletons quiver in the closet
    a couple of almost friends who're now grandparents, sometimes bilious at other times saccharine who carry, without it apparently weighing them down at first sight, several criminal records for embezzlement, harassment of minors or adults, who defend at any price that doing children doesn't necessarily imply corruption because the Greeks and Foucault and Gide and blah blah blah
    neither colleges nor associations, no one makes great waves, prestige
              obliges
    and sends them home, they circulate that there's nothing to see
ladies and gentlemen
place your bets
black zero

"Hay adolescentes que desean los abusos, incluso te provocan", insistió el Bernardo Alvarez, obispo de Tenerife, un 28 de diciembre, creedme
    créanme
    si lo dice la Iglesia, metro patrón del orden y sosiego
    qué nos queda a nuestras agencias, escuelitas
    y ministerios defensores de la viuda y del menor
    hacer la vista gorda
    brindemos a Moloch nuestros hjitos más desharrapados
    desvíen señoras y señores el paso y la mirada
    ¿colonialista, hijo de puta, gran bonete, yo?

    campo
    cereales alumnos en silos
    carreteras del purgatorio
    ohio, el mundo

"There are teenagers who want to be abused, they even provoke it", insisted Bernardo Alvarez, Bishop of Tenerife, one 28th December, believe me

    believe me
    if the Church doth so declare, chief ruler of order and calm
    what is left for our agencies, schools
    and ministries, defenders of widows and minors
    to turn a blind eye
    hand our most ragged offspring over to Moloch
    ladies and gentlemen please avert your gaze and divert your path
    colonialist, son of a bitch, Mr. Nobody, *me*?

    countryside
    students like cereals in silos
    highways of purgatory
    Ohio, the world

transporte público no hay
uno se acostumbra
el café aguado en tazones de papel encerado
con pajita
las ventanas selladas
me ahogo
uno se acostumbra
¿los negros pueden disfrutar de la sombra de un árbol central?
el árbol LUCA del bien y del mal,
en pleno campus
el temporal, tanto cierzo, cómo joden
todavía

casas grandes para gente aún más grande amante de las miniaturas
las carreras de embolsados
las luces fluorescentes y las tartas de zapallo

meta: hilvanar con hilo de nylon invisible el embrollo
separar la paja del heno
qué es segmento
y cuán intangible
la pinche realidad

there's no public transport
you get used to it
watered-down coffee in lidded paper cups
with a straw
windows sealed
I choke
you get used to it
can the black people enjoy the shade of a tree in the centre?
The LUCA tree of good and evil,
mid-campus
the rough weather, blustering north wind, how they still
pester

large houses for even larger people who're avid collectors of miniatures
egg and spoon races
fluorescent lights and pumpkin pies

goal: to bundle the hotchpotch together with invisible nylon thread
separate the straw from the hay
what's fragment
and how intangible
tight-fisted reality is

en el banco de gambier, ohio
una rubia que ni dibujada por hammett y por carver
pelo rizado mechones platino y berenjena
detrás de una ventanilla con forma de azucarado medallón
cuenta billetes color bilis
a la noche un grandote de los que frecuenta
entre bourbon y bourbon le dirá *baby don't cry*
y le tenderá un kleenex –gran invento– para sorber los humores
del ánima y del cosmos, y ya vuelta en sí
pensará que es hora de volver a esmaltarse las uñas de los pies

in the bank in Gambier, Ohio
a blond, curly hair, platinum and *aubergine* locks
whom neither Hammett nor Carver have drawn
behind a window shaped like a sherbet medallion
counts bile-colored notes
at night one of those large fellows she frequents
will say to her, in between one bourbon and another, *baby don't cry*
and he'll hold out a paper handkerchief—wonderful invention—to
      snuffle the moods
of her soul and the cosmos, and once again absorbed in herself
she'll think that it's about time she touched up the polish on her toenails

por la calle un carro
con pareja de amish de tarjeta postal
sus nenas tiesitas de cuello alado blanco
él luenga barba grisácea y riendas sobadas
no tengo siquiera una sonrisa de circunstancias
ni curiosidad por nuestros mutuos disfraces
anacrónicos
los abandono
nos dejamos trotar

a cart in the street
carrying a picture postcard Amish couple
their upright little girls with their white winged collars
him with a long greyish beard and shabby reins
I don't even wear a forced or curious smile
about our mutual
anachronic
costumes
I abscond
we leave one another on the trot

Capa poblacional que descubro: la de los eméritos.
Condición mirífica a la que aspiro con envidia y avidez
y qué oficio le pondremos exigía una ronda infantil
como querer quiero levantarme una mañana y ser como los nombran
en japón, TNV –Tesoro Nacional Viviente–, en alguna tierra donde no
hayan florecido ni campos de exterminio ni gulags, ni guerras
todas sucias derrotas, a más no poder
ergo levantarme en ninguna parte

Pero el periódico me obliga
a que NO deje de lado, fuera de la memoria
algo que los nazis ni siquiera soñaron
o a lo mejor sí y lo perpetraron sunitas y chiítas;
tomaron hoy a dos mujeres mongólicas, *las locas del mercado*
El saldo, cien muertos, ellas las primeras.
Mientras sunitas y chiítas a la hora del muezzin
peroran tomando té con menta y bizcochitos caseros
con mucha miel

I discover a sector of the population: those who are emeritus.
A learned condition to which I aspire with envy and desire
and what occupation shall we give her chanted the circle of singing
          children
    as a wish I want to get up in the morning and be what they call in
Japan a LNT—Living National Treasure—to arise in a country in which
neither extermination camps nor gulags nor wars have flourished
    all defeats, as dirty as can be
    ergo get up nowhere

    But the newspaper forces me
    NOT to leave to one side, out of mind
    something that not even the Nazis dreamt of
    or chances are they did, but the Sunnis and Shi'ites perpetrated
    today they took women with Down's syndrome, *the mad women of*
            the marketplace
    The balance sheet: 100 dead, they were the first
    while Sunnis and Shi'ites
    converse at the hour of muezzin as they drink mint tea and snack
           on little homemade cakes
    with lots of honey

En mis clases hablo de romanticismo
ante un decano mormón o anabaptista
que duerme estrepitoso en primera fila
y me desconcierto avergonzada
estamos a mil ochocientos metros de altura y boqueo
adiós everest, adiós aconcagua que otros escalarán con mi tea
y mis ganas de vivir infiltradas cada vez más de mis ganas de morir

In my classes I talk about romanticism
before an Anabaptist or Mormon Dean
who dozes noisily in the front row
and I become ashamedly bewildered
we're at 1,800 meters above sea level and I utter
goodbye Everest, farewell Aconcagua which others will climb with
                my firebrand
and my will to live increasingly shot through with my will to die

adiós al junco y al sampán
caricias centro mismo de la intimidad adiós

única certidumbre
polvo eres

En realidad
siempre lo supe
tendrán que seguir abanicándose
perdiendo aguas
en un mundo sin mí.

so long Junco and Sampan
caresses, the very centre of intimacy, so long

the only certainty
is that you're dust

In truth
I always knew that
you'll have to continue fanning yourselves
waters breaking
in a world without me.

www.ingramcontent.com/pod-product-compliance
Lightning Source LLC
Chambersburg PA
CBHW021327190426
43193CB00039B/350